A KEY TO THE FUNDAMENTALS OF GW-BASIC PROGRAMMING

FROM SIMPLE PROGRAMS TO LOOPS AND STRINGS

PRITMA JASHNANI

ISBN 979-888629199-5

I dedicate this book to the students who are ready to learn programming and try programs on their own.The answers given in this book will help them check their programs.

Contents

Preface

When Programming starts at Schools, Children are first taught LOGO, Scratch and BASIC .Since BASIC is the first step to learn decision making statements and looping .This book has given step by step guide to the students.

This is an answer book to all the exercises given in **THE FUNDAMENTALS OF GW- BASIC PROGRAMMING BOOK**

While solving exercises, if you do find difficulty, please mail on the email address.

jashpritma@gmail.com

Acknowledgements

I express my sincere gratitude to my late mother, late brother, my father and my sisters, without whom it was not possible to express my thoughts in the form of words written in this book.

Though my mother is not with us, but her blessings and love always remains with us. She had a belief that one day I will be writing books and become an author.

I also express my gratitude to my mentor **Inspiring Jatin** under whose guidance, I could actually make my wish of becoming an author come true.

About The Author

Pritma Jashnani, is the head of **Centre of Computer Technology**, Lucknow, who has taught several students so far in her career of 25 years.

She has taught more than 3000+ students who are now successfully placed in top companies. She has a unique style of teaching. She believes in quality education rather than increasing quantity of students.

She has been teaching courses like

Java, Website Designing, Data Structures, Python, Android and a lot more to B.Tech, MCA and BCA students.

13 years back, she started writing books for her students so that they do not find any difficulty in the topics they are taught.

She took a lot of time doing research and picking questions from the exam papers of various schools and compiling them into set of two both for class 10th and 12th.

Study Material and Exercise book.

She has also written books on **ASP.NET, PHP, PYTHON, Core Java, C#, Advanced Java, Oracle etc.**

This book has been made as an answer book to **FUNDAMENTALS OF GW- BASIC PROGRAMMING BOOK** for students studying in class VI, VII AND VIII, so that if at any point they get stuck they can use this book for reference. This can also be of help to Teachers who are teaching Basic at Schools.

Hope you like this book as it will encourage her to write more books for you.

A. For Joining any courses ,you can contact her by sending mail on jashpritma@gmail.com

You can even buy any study materials on **Java, ANDROID, ASP.NET, C,C++,C#,PHP etc.**

CHAPTER ONE

ANSWERS TO EXERCISE BASED ON LESSON 1

EXERCISES FOR YOU

1. LET B=2.4
2. A$="DELHI"
3. B$=A$
4. A=(A+B)
5. A=A-10

Fill in the blanks

1. **Program to print value of A and B and also calculate their product**

```
10 LET A=5
20 LET B=10
30 PRINT A,B
40 LET C=A*B
50 PRINT C
60 END
```

1. **To Print the numbers and their sum on the same line**

```
10 LET A=5
20 LET B=10
30 PRINT A,B,A+B
40 END
```

3. **Modify the above program such that it gives the output : THE PRODUCT IS 50**

```
50 PRINT "THE PRODUCT IS",C
```

PROGRAMS PRACTICE

1. 10 INPUT N

```
20 LET B=N mod 10
30 LET C=N/10
```

```
40 PRINT "FIRST DIGIT=",C
50 PRINT "LAST DIDGIT=",B
60 END
```

2. 10 INPUT C

```
20 F=(C/5)*9+32
30 PRINT "FAHRENHEIT=",F
40 END
```

3. 10 INPUT A,B

```
20 PRINT A+B
30 PRINT A-B
40 PRINT A*B
50 PRINT A/B
60 END
```

4. 10 INPUT "Enter radius",R

```
20 LET A=22/7*R^2
30 LET C=2*22/7*R
40 PRINT "AREA=",A
50 PRINT "CIRCUMFERENCE=",C
60 END
```

5. 10 INPUT "PRINCIPAL,RATE AND TIME",P,R,T

```
20 LET SI=(P*R*T)/100
30 PRINT "SIMPLE INTEREST=".SI
40 END
```

6. 10 INPUT "ENTER NUMBER AND POWER",N,P

```
20 PRINT N^P
30 END
```

7. 10 INPUT L,B,H

```
20 LET V=L*B*H
30 PRINT "VOLUME=",V
40 END
```

GIVE OUTPUT

1. 10 LET X=2*(3+4) = 14
2. 10 LET X=1^2^3 =1
3. 10 LET X=(1+2)^3 =27
4. 10 LET X=1*2^3 =8

5. 10 LET X=2^(3^2)=512

CORRECT THE PROGRAMS

1. **PROGRAM TO ENTER NAME AND CLASS**

```
10 LET N$="ANUP"
20 LET C$="6A"
30 PRINT N$,C$
40 END
```

2. **Program to calculate Quotient**

```
10 LET A
20 INPUT B=2
30 PRINT A/B
40 END
```

3. **Program to enter Name and marks of 2 subjects and print Total and Name.**

```
10 INPUT N$
20 INPUT M1,M2
30 LET T=M1+M2
40 PRINT N$,T
50 END
```

IDENTIFY THE CORRECT STRING VARIABLES.

1. N$ 2. C 4. Z$3 4. Z3$

The correct answers are

1. N$ 4. Z3$

CHAPTER TWO

ANSWERS TO EXERCISES BASED ON CHAPTER 2

1. 10 INPUT N

```
20 IF N MOD 7=0 OR N MOD 10=7 THEN PRINT "BUZZ NUMBER" ELSE PRINT "NOT BUZZ
NUMBER"
30 END
2. 10 INPUT "ENTER 2 NUMBERS",A,B
20 IF A>B THEN PRINT A-B ELSE PRINT B-A
30 END
```

3. 10 INPUT"ENTER INCOME",S

```
20 IF S<=130000 THEN TAX=0
30 IF S>130000 AND S<=200000 THEN TAX=(15*(S-130000)/100)
40 IF S>200000 AND S<=250000 THEN TAX=5000+(20*(S-200000)/100)
50 IF S>250000 THEN TAX=(30*(S-250000)/100)
60 PRINT TAX
70 END
```

4. 10 INPUT "TOTAL COST",C

```
20 IF C<=2000 THEN D=(5*C)/100
30 IF C>2001 AND C<=5000 THEN D=(25*C)/100
40 IF C>=5001 AND C<=10000 THEN D=(35*C)/100
50 IF C>10000 THEN D=(50*C)/100
60 AMOUNT=C-D
70 PRINT "AMOUNT TO PAY=",AMOUNT
80 END
```

5. 10 INPUT SALES

```
20 IF SALES>100000 THEN COMM=(25*SALES)/100
30 IF SALES>80000 AND SALES<=100000 THEN COMM=(22.5*SALES)/100
40 IF SALES>=60000 AND SALES<80000 THEN COMM=(20*SALES)/100
50 IF SALES>=40000 AND SALES<60000 THEN COMM=(15*SALES)/100
```

60 IF SALES<40000 THEN COMM=(12.5*SALES)/100
70 PRINT COMM
80 END

6. 10 INPUT "ENTER MARKS OF 3 SUBJECTS",M1,M2,M3

   20 LET AVG=(M1+M2+M3)/3
   30 IF AVG>80 THEN PRINT "GRADE A"
   40 IF AVG>=60 AND AVG<=79 THEN PRINT "GRADE B"
   50 IF AVG>=50 AND AVG<=59 THEN PRINT "GRADE C"
   60 IF AVG>=40 AND AVG<=49 THEN PRINT "GRADE D"
   70 IF AVG<40 THEN PRINT "FAIL"
   80 END

7. 10 INPUT "ENTER 3 SIDES OF A TRIANGLE",A,B,C

   20 IF A*A=B^2+C^2 OR B^2=A*A+C*C OR C^2=A^2+B^2 THEN PRINT "RIGHT ANGLED TRIANGLE" ELSE PRINT "NOT RIGHT ANGLED"
   30 END

8. 10 INPUT "SALARY=",SAL

   20 IF SAL>15000 THEN HRA=(10*SAL)/100
   30 IF SAL>=10000 AND SAL<=15000 THEN HRA=(15*SAL)/100
   40 IF SAL>15000 THEN HRA=(20*SAL)/100
   50 PRINT "HRA=",HRA
   60 END

9. 10 INPUT N

   20 IF N>=0 AND N<=9 THEN PRINT "SINGLE DIGIT NUMBER"
   30 IF N>=10 AND N<=99 THEN PRINT "TWO DIGIT NUMBER"
   40 IF N>100 AND N<=999 THEN PRINT "THREE DIGIT NUMBER"
   50 END

10. 10 INPUT C$

    20 IF C$="A" OR C$="E" OR C$="I" OR C$="O" OR C$="U" THEN PRINT "IT IS A VOWEL" ELSE PRINT "IT IS A CONSONANT"
    30 END

11. 10 INPUT "ENTER MONTH NUMBER",M

    20 IF M=12 OR M=1 OR M=2 THEN PRINT "WINTER"
    30 IF M=3 OR M=4 OR M=5 THEN PRINT "SPRING"
    40 IF M=6 OR M=7 OR M=8 THEN PRINT "SUMMER"
    50 IF M=9 OR M=10 OR M=11 THEN PRINT "AUTUMN"

60 END

12. 10 INPUT “ENTER A NUMBER”

    20 IF N>0 AND N MOD 2=0 THEN PRINT “POSITIVE
    EVEN”
    30 IF N>0 AND N MOD 2<>0 THEN PRINT “POSITIVE
    ODD”
    40 IF N<0 AND N MOD 2=0 THEN PRINT “NEGATIVE EVEN” ELSE PRINT “NEGATIVE ODD”
    50 END

13. 10 PRINT “1. AREA OF RECTANGLE”

    20 PRINT “2. AREA OF SQUARE”
    30 INPUT “ENTER CHOICE”,C
    40 IF C=1 THEN GOTO 60
    50 IF C=2 THEN GOTO 80
    60 INPUT L,B
    70 PRINT “AREA=”,L*B:GOTO 100
    80 INPUT “ENTER SIDE”,S
    90 PRINT “AREA=”,S*S
    100 END

14. 10 INPUT “UNITS”,U

    20 IF U<=100 THEN B=U*1.50+250
    30 IF U>100 AND U<=200 THEN B=100*1.50+(U-
    100)*2.00+250
    40 IF U>200 AND U<=250 THEN B = 100 * 1.50 +
    100*2.00+(U-200)*2.50+250
    50 IF U>250 THEN B=100*1.50+100*2.00+ 50*2.50 +
    (U-250)*4.00+250
    60 PRINT “BILL=”,B
    70 END

15. 10 INPUT “ENTER CHARACTER”,C$

    20 IF C$=”C” THEN PRINT “CHAIRMAN”
    30 IF C$=”D” THEN PRINT “DIRECTOR”
    40 IF C$=”M” THEN PRINT “MANAGER”
    50 END

16. 10 INPUT N

    20 IF N MOD 10=9 AND N MOD 6=0 THEN PRINT
    “SPECIAL NUMBER” ELSE PRINT “NOT SPECIAL”
    30 END

17. 10 INPUT "YEAR",Y

    20 IF Y MOD 100=0 AND Y MOD 400=0 OR Y MOD 4=0 THEN PRINT "LEAP YEAR" ELSE PRINT "NOT A LEAP YEAR"
    30 END

18. 10 INPUT "ENTER NAME",N$

    20 INPUT "ENTER MARKS OF 3 SUBJECTS",P,C,M
    30 LET T=P+C+M
    40 IF P>70 AND C>80 AND M>90 AND T>=250 THEN PRINT N$,"YOU GET SCIENCE" ELSE PRINT N$,"YOU DO NOT GET SCIENCE"
    50 END

Give output

1. I) If A$="AMIT" N=20

   ?"AMIT",20
   AMIT YOU CAN VOTE
   Ready

ii. If A$="NUPUR" N=15

   ?"NUPUR",15
   NUPUR YOU CANNOT VOTE
   Ready

2. **2.5**

   Ready

3. I) If VAL=1000,N=2000

   ?1000,2000
   200
   Ready

i. IF VAL=500,N=1500

   ?500,1500
   200
   Ready

ii. IF VAL=600 ,N=2500

   ?600,2500
   400

Ready

CHAPTER THREE

ANSWERS TO EXERCISE BASED ON CHAPTER 3

GIVE OUTPUTS

1. REM ** PROGRAM

```
10 LET A=5
20 WHILE A<=25
30 PRINT A*2
40 A=A+3
50 WEND
60 END
Run
```

10
16
22
28
34
40
46
Ready

1. REM **PROGRAM

```
10 LET I=5
20 F=1:S=0
30 J=1
40 WHILE J<=I
50 F=F*J
60 S=S+F
70 J=J+1
80 WEND
90 PRINT S
100 END
RUN
```

153
Ready

3. REM ** PROGRAM

```
10 M=10:N=7
20 WHILE M MOD N>0
30 LET M=M+1
40 LET N=N+2
50 PRINT M,N
60 WEND
70 END
RUN
```

11 9
12 11
13 13
Ready

4. REM ** PROGRAM

```
10 LET COUNT=3
20 WHILE COUNT<>0
30 PRINT COUNT
40 COUNT=COUNT+3
50 WEND
```

RUN
3
6
9
.
.
Infinity
Ready

5. REM **PROGRAM

```
10 LET N$="HELLO"
20 LET I=2
30 WHILE I<=10
40 PRINT N$,I
50 I=I+2
60 WEND
70 END
RUN
```

HELLO 2
HELLO 4
HELLO 6
HELLO 8
HELLO 10
Ready

6. REM **PROGRAM

```
10 LET M=5
20 WHILE M<=15
30 PRINT "*",
40 M=M+2
50 WEND
RUN
* * * * * *
Ready
```

7. REM **RPOGRAM

```
10 LET P=2
20 WHILE P<=20
30 PRINT P,P*3
40 P=P+1
50 WEND
60 END
RUN
2 6
3 9
4 12
5 15
6 18
7 21
8 24
9 27
10 30
11 33
12 36
13 39
14 42
15 45
16 48
17 51
18 54
19 57
20 60
Ready
```

8. REM **PROGRAM

```
10 X=1000:Y=9
20 Z=5
30 WHILE X>=Y
40 X=X/Y
50 Z=Z+1
```

```
60 WEND
70 PRINT Z
80 END
Run
8
Ready
```

9. REM **PROGRAM

```
10 N=345
20 WHILE N>0
30 R=N MOD 10
40 IF R MOD 2=0 THEN SUM=SUM+R
50 N=N/10
60 WEND
70 PRINT SUM
```

80. END

```
RUN
4
Ready
```

10. REM ** PROGRAM

```
10 LET X=20:Y=30
20 WHILE X<Y
30 Y=Y-1
40 PRINT Y
50 X=X+1
60 WEND
70 PRINT X
80 END
RUN
29
28
27
26
25
25
Ready
```

Questions on Programming

1. 10 INPUT A,B

```
20 I=1
30 IF A>B THEN L=A ELSE L=B
30 While I<=L
```

```
40 IF A MOD I=0 AND B MOD I=0 THEN HCF=I
50 I=I+1
60 WEND
70 PRINT "HCF=";HCF
80 END
```

2. 10 INPUT L

```
20 A=0:B=1
30 I=1
40 WHILE I<=L
50 C=A+B
60 PRINT C;
70 A=B
80 B=C
90 I=I+1
100 WEND
110 END
```

3. 10 INPUT L

```
20 A=1:B=1:C=2
30 I=1
40 WHILE I<=L
50 D=A+B+C
60 PRINT D;
70 A=B
80 B=C
90 C=D
100 I=I+1
110 WEND
120 END
```

4. 10 INPUT N

```
20 M=N:P=1
30 WHILE N>0
40 R=N MOD 10
50 S=S+R
60 P=P*R
70 N=(N-R)/10
80 WEND
90 IF M=S+P THEN PRINT "SPECIAL 2 DIGIT NUMBER" ELSE PRINT "NOT"
100 END
```

5. 10 INPUT N

```
20 I=1
```

```
30 WHILE I<N
40 IF N MOD I=0 THEN C=C+I
50 I=I+1
60 WEND
70 IF C=N THEN PRINT "PERFECT NUMBER" ELSE PRINT "NOT PERFECT"
80 END
```

6. 10 INPUT

```
20 I=1
30 WHILE I<=N
40 S=S+I
50 T=T+S
60 I=I+2
70 WEND
80 PRINT T
90 END
```

7. 10 INPUT N

```
20 M=N*N:Y=N
30 WHILE N>0
40 C=C+1
50 N=N/10
60 WEND
70 IF M MOD 10^C =Y THEN PRINT "AUTOMORPHIC" ELSE PRINT "NOT AUTOMORPHIC"
80 END
```

8. 10 INPUT N

```
20 I=2
30 WHILE I<=N
40 S=S+I/(I*2)
50 I=I+1
60 WEND
70 PRINT S
80 END
```

9. 10 I=1

```
20 WHILE I<=10
30 INPUT N$,AV
40 IF AV>80 THEN PRINT N$,AV:C=C+1
50 I=I+1
60 WEND
70 PRINT C
80 END
```

10. 10 I=1

```
20 WHILE I<=10
30 INPUT N
40 IF N<0 AND N MOD 2=0 THEN C=C+1
50 IF N<0 AND N MOD 2<>0 THEN D=D+1
60 IF N>0 AND N MOD 2=0 THEN E=E+1
70 IF N>0 AND N MOD 2<>0 THEN F=F+1
80 I=I+1
90 WEND
100 PRINT C,D,E,F
110 END
```

11. 10 INPUT N

```
20 M=N
30 WHILE N>0
40 R=N MOD 10
50 S=S+R^3
60 N=(N-R)/10
70 WEND
80 IF M=S THEN PRINT “ARMSTRONG NUMBER” ELSE
PRINT “NOT ARMSTRONG”
90 END
```

12. 10 INPUT N

```
20 I=1
30 WHILE I<=10
40 PRINT N*I
50 I=I+1
60 WEND
70 END
```

13. 10 INPUT N

```
20 I=1
30 WHILE I<=N
40 PRINT I*I*I-1
50 I=I+1
60 WEND
70 END
```

14. 10 I=1

```
20 INPUT N
30 WHILE I<=N
40 INPUT AGE
```

```
50 IF AGE>=26 AND AGE<=35 THEN C=C+1
60 IF AGE>=36 AND AGE<=45 THEN D=D+1
70 IF AGE>=46 AND AGE<=55 THEN E=E+1
80 I=I+1
90 WEND
100 PRINT "AGE 26-35=",C
110 PRINT "AGE 36-45=",D
120 PRINT "AGE 46-55=",E
130 END
```

15.

```
10 INPUT N

20 M=N*N
30 WHILE M>0
40 R=M MOD 10
50 S=S+R
60 M=(M-R)/10
70 WEND
80 IF S=N THEN PRINT "NEON NUMBER"
ELSE PRINT "NOT NEON"
90 END
```

16.

```
10 INPUT N

20 M=N
30 WHILE N>0
40 R=N MOD 10
50 S=S+R
60 N=(N-R)/10
70 WEND
80 IF M MOD S=0 THEN PRINT "NIVEN" ELSE PRINT "NOT
NIVEN"
```

CHAPTER FOUR

ANWERS TO EXERCISE BASED ON CHAPTER 4

Give output

1. FOR I=1 to 10 Step 3

PRINT I,
NEXT
RUN
1 4 7 10
Ready

1. FOR I=10 to 1 Step -4

PRINT I*2,
NEXT
RUN
20 12 4
Ready

3.

10. FOR I=5 to 20 STEP 5

20 IF I MOD 3=0 THEN GOTO 50
30 IF I MOD 5=0 THEN PRINT I
40 NEXT
50 END
RUN
5
10
Ready

4. 10 LET N=7

20 FOR I=1 to N
30 IF N MOD I =0 THEN C=C+1
40 NEXT I

50 IF C=2 THEN PRINT “PRIME” ELSE PRINT “NOT PRIME”
60 END
RUN
7
PRIME
Ready

5. 10 LET N=3

20 FOR I=1 to 5
30 PRINT N^I,
40 NEXT I

50. END

RUN
3 9 27 81 243
Ready

6. 10 FOR I= 1 to 10

20 PRINT I,I^2,I^3
30 NEXT I
40 END
RUN
1 1 1
2 4 8
3 9 27
4 16 64
5 25 125
6 36 216
7 49 343
8 64 512
9 81 729
10 100 1000
Ready

7. 10 FOR I=3 to 10 step 3

20 PRINT I/2,
30 NEXT I
40 END
RUN
1.5
3
4.5
Ready
PROGRAMS TO PRACTICE

1. ```
   10 INPUT N

   20 FOR I=1 TO N/2
   30 IF N MOD I =0 THEN PRINT I
   40 NEXT I
   50 END
   ```

2. ```
   10 A=1:B=1:C=0

   20 INPUT N
   30 FOR I=1 TO N
   40 LET D=A+B+C
   50 PRINT D
   60 A=B
   70 B=C
   80 C=D
   90 NEXT I
   100 END
   ```

3. ```
   10 INPUT N

   20 FOR I=2 TO N STEP 2
   30 S=S+I
   40 T=T+S
   50 NEXT I
   60 END
   70 PRINT T
   80 END
   ```

4. ```
   10 INPUT N

   20 FOR I=2 TO N
   30 S=S+I/(I*2)+1
   40 NEXT I
   50 PRINT S
   60 END
   ```

5. ```
   10 INPUT N

   20 FOR I=1 TO N/2
   30 IF N MOD I =0 THEN PRINT S=S+I
   40 NEXT I
   50 IF S=N THEN PRINT “PERFECT NUMBER” ELSE PRINT “NOT PERFECT”
   50 END
   ```

6. ```
   10 FOR I=1 TO 10

   20 INPUT L,B
   ```

```
30 LET AREA=L*B
40 LET PERI=2*(L+B)
50 PRINT AREA,PERI
60 NEXT I
70 END
```

7.
```
10 FOR I=1 TO 10

20 INPUT N$,A
30 IF A>18 THEN PRINT N$,A
40 NEXT I
50 END
```

8.
```
10 FOR I=1 TO 10

20 INPUT N
30 IF N<0 AND N MOD 2=0 THEN C=C+1
40 IF N<0 AND N MOD 2<>0 THEN D=D+1
50 IF N>0 AND N MOD 2=0 THEN E=E+1
60 IF N>0 AND N MOD 2<> 0 THEN F=F+1
70 NEXT I
80 PRINT “NEGATIVE EVEN”,C
90 PRINT “NEGATIVE ODD”,D
100 PRINT “POSITIIVE EVEN”,E
110 PRINT “POSITIVE ODD”,F
120 END
```

9.
```
10 FOR I=10 TO 100

20 C=0
30 FOR J=1 TO I
40 IF I MOD J=0 THEN C=C+1
50 NEXT J
60 IF C=2 THEN PRINT I
70 NEXT I
80 END
```

10.
```
10 FOR I=1 TO 20

20 INPUT AGE
30 IF AGE>=26 AND AGE<=35 THEN C=C+1
40 IF AGE>=36 AND AGE<=45 THEN D=D+1
50 IF AGE>=46 AND AGE<=55 THEN E=E+1
60 NEXT I
70 PRINT “26-35=”,C
80 PRINT “36-45=”,D
90 PRINT “46-55=”,E
100 END
```

CHAPTER FIVE

ANSWERS TO EXERCISES ON CHAPTER 5

Programs

1. 10 FOR I=10 TO 100

```
20 C=0
30 FOR J=1 TO I
40 IF I MOD J=0 THEN C=C+1
50 NEXT J
60 IF C=2 THEN PRINT I
70 NEXT I
```

1. END

2. 10 FOR I=10 TO 500

```
20 C=0:N=I
30 FOR J=1 TO 3
40 R= N MOD 10
50 C=C+R^3
60 N=(N-R)/10
70 NEXT J
60 IF C=I THEN PRINT I
70 NEXT I
80 END
```

3. 10 FOR I= 1 TO 5

```
20 FOR J=1 TO I
30 IF J MOD 2<>0 THEN PRINT "*" ELSE PRINT "#";
40 NEXT J
50 PRINT
60 NEXT I
```

70. ND

4. 10 FOR I=65 TO 69

   20 FOR J=69 TO I STEP -1
   30 PRINT CHR$(I);
   40 NEXT J
   50 PRINT
   60 NEXT I
   70 END

5. 10 FOR I=5 TO 1 STEP -1

   20 FOR J=5 TO I STEP -1
   30 PRINT J;
   40 NEXT J
   50 PRINT
   60 NEXT I
   70 END

6. 10 FOR I=69 TO 65 STEP -1

   20 FOR K=68 TO I STEP -1
   30 PRINT " ";
   40 NEXT K
   50 FOR J=I TO 65 STEP -1
   60 PRINT CHR$(J);
   70 NEXT J
   80 PRINT
   90 NEXT I
   100 END

7. 10 K=1

   20FOR I=65 TO 68
   30 FOR J=65 TO J
   40 PRINT CHR$(J);K;
   50 K=K+1
   60 NEXT J
   70 PRINT
   80 K=1
   90 NEXT I
   100 END

8. 10 K=1

   20 FOR I=1 TO 4
   30 FOR K=3 TO I STEP -1
   40 PRINT " ";
   50 NEXT K

```
60 FOR J=1 TO I
70 PRINT K;
80 K=K+2
90 NEXT J
100 PRINT
110 NEXT I
120 END
```

9. 10 FOR I= 2 TO 10 STEP 2

```
20 FOR K=2 TO I-2 STEP 2
30 PRINT " ";
40 NEXT K
50 FOR J=I TO 10 STEP 2
60 PRINT J;
70 NEXT J
80 PRINT
90 NEXT I
100 END
```

10. 10 FOR I=20 TO 100

```
20 C=0
30 FOR J=1 TO I/2
40 IF I MOD J=0 THEN C=C+I
50 NEXT J
60 IF C=I THEN PRINT I
70 NEXT I
80 END
```

CORRECT THE FOLLOWING PROGRAMS AND REWRITE

1. 05 REM PRINT 1 to 10

```
10 FOR I=1 TO 10
20 PRINT I
40 NEXT I
```

2. 05 REM LOOP NESTING

```
10 FOR I=1 TO 10
20 FOR J=1 TO 6
30 PRINT J
40 NEXT J
50 PRINT
50 NEXT I
```

3. 05 REM PRINTING SQUARE FOR EVEN NOS 2 TO 10

```
10 for K=2 TO 10 STEP 2
20 PRINT K
30 PRINT K*K
40 NEXT K
```

4. 10 REM PRINT YOUR NAME 5 TIMES

```
20 INPUT"NAME";N$
30 FOR I=1 TO 5
40 PRINT N$
50 NEXT I
```

5. 10 REM PRINT MULTIPLICATION TABLE FROM 1 TO 10 OF A NUMBER

```
20 INPUT N
30 FOR I=1 TO 10
40 PRINT N*I
50 NEXT I
60 END
```

FILL IN THE BLANKS

1. 10 REM PRINTING NUMBER 1 TO 10

20 FOR N=1 TO 10
30 PRINT N
40 **NEXT N**
50 END

2. 10 REM PRINTING ODD NOS 1 TO 19

20FOR N=**1 TO 9 STEP 2**
30 PRINT N
40 NEXT N
50 STOP

3. 10 REM GENERATE NOS 1 TO 9 IN DESCENDING ORDER

20 FOR N=9 TO 1 STEP -2
30 PRINT N
40 NEXT N
50 STOP

4. 10 REM PRINT * 5 TIMES IN A LINE

20 FOR I=**1 TO 5**
30 PRINT "*";
40 NEXT I
50 STOP

5. 10 REM PRINTING TRIANGLE LIKE

```
20 FOR I=1 TO 3
30 FOR J=1 TO I
40 PRINT "*";
50 NEXT J
60 PRINT
70 NEXT I
80 STOP
```

CHAPTER SIX

ANSWERS TO EXERCISES BASED ON CHAPTER 6 AND CHAPTER 7

Write Statements for the following

1. Assign a value BOMBAY to a String variable A$.

   LET A$="BOMBAY"

1. Find the total number of characters present in the variable A$.

   PRINT LEN(A$)

3. Extract 4 characters from the right of the string A$

   PRINT RIGHT$(A$,4)

4. Extract 3 characters starting from 2nd position of the string

   PRINT MID$(A$,2,3)

5. Concatenate the string variable A$ with "CITY"

   A$=A$+"CITY"

6. Find absolute value of the variable N having a value -30.4

   LET N=-30.4
   PRINT ABS(N)

7. Convert the value "345" stored in a string B$ to an integer value.

   LET B$="345"
   PRINT VAL(B$)

8. Give the integer part of the value 34.566.

   PRINT INT(34.566)

9. Give the square root of the value 49.

   PRINT SQR(49)

10. Find the square and cube of value 4.

    PRINT 4^2
    PRINT 4^3
    Give output

1. PRINT CHR$(109)

   ANS : m

2. PRINT ASC("p")

   ANS: 112

3. 10 LET H$="HELLO"

   20 PRINT ASC(H$)
   ANS: 72

4. PRINT FIX(45.7)

   ANS: 45

5. PRINT ROUND(34.56,1)

   ANS: 35

6. PRINT LEFT$(H$,2)+RIGHT$(H$,2)

   ANS: HELO

7. PRINT MID$("CLOUD",1,3)

   ANS: LOU
   FILL IN THE BLANKS

1. PROGRAM TO PRINT ONLY NUMERIC VALUE

   10 D$="10 OCTOBER"
   20 DD=VAL(D$)
   30 PRINT DD
 40 END

2. PROGRAM TO PRINT AGE VALUE ONLY

```
10 INPUT "ENTER YOUR AGE";A$
20 Y=VAL (A$)
30 PRINT Y
40 END
```

3. PROGRAM TO FIND DIFFERENCE IN TWO NUMBERS

```
10 A$="15 IS THE FIRST NUMBER"
20 B$="10 IS THE SECOND NUMBER"
30 M=VAL(A$)
40 N=VAL(B$)
50 Y=M-N
60 PRINT "DIFFERENCE OF TWO NUMBERS IS";Y
```

4. PROGRAM TO FIND LENGTH OF A STRING

```
10 INPUT "ENTER A STRING";A$
20 L=LEN(A$)
30 PRINT "THE LENGTH IS";L
```

5. PROGRAM TO PRINT DATE AS 18/09/22

```
10 INPUT "ENTER DATE";DD,MM,YY
20 D$=STR$(DD)
30 M$=STR$(MM)
40Y$=STR$(YY)
50 A$=D$+"/"M$+"/"+Y$
60 PRINT A$
```

6. PROGRAM TO PRINT LAST 6 LETTERS AND 12 TO 14 LETTERS

```
10 A$="MY NAME IS RIP VAN WINKLE"
20 LET B$=RIGHT$(A$,6)
30 C$=MID$(A$,12,3)
40 D$=B$+C$
50 PRINT D$
60 END
```

CORRECT THE FOLLOWING

1. PROGRAM TO CONVERT INTEGER TO STRING

```
10 A=405
20 A1$=STR$(A)
30 PRINT A1$
40 END
```

2. PROGRAM TO CONVERT WEIGHT IN LBS TO KGS

```
10 INPUT "ENTER WEIGHT IN LBS",W1$
20 W=VAL(W1$)
30 PRINT W/2.2;"KGS"
40 END
```

3. PROGRAM TO EXTRACT CHARACTERS FROM LEFT

```
10 A$="GREAT"
20 L=LEN(A$)
30 FOR I=1 TO L
40 PRINT LEFT$(A$,I)
50 NEXT I
60 END
```

4. PROGRAM TO GET OUTPUT AS DD

```
10 A$="AA BB CC DD"
20 B$=RIGHT$(A$,2)
30 PRINT B$
40 END
```

Write Programs

1. 10 INPUT A$

```
20 L=LEN(A$)
30 FOR I=1 TO L
40 FOR J=1 TO I
50 PRINT MID$(A$,I,1);
60 NEXT J
70 PRINT
80 NEXT I
90 END
```

2. 10 INPUT A$

```
20 L=LEN(A$)
30 FOR I=1 TO L
40 C$=MID$(A$,I,1)
50 IF C$>="0" AND C$<="9" THEN SUM=SUM+INT(C$)
60 NEXT I
70 PRINT SUM
80 END
```

3. 10 INPUT A$

20. FOR I=65 TO 90

```
30 FOR J=1 TO LEN(A$)
```

```
40 C$=MID$(A$,J,1)
50 IF C$=CHR$(I) THEN D=D+1
60 NEXT J
70 IF D!=0 THEN PRINT CHR$(I);"OCCURRED",D; "TIMES"
80 D=0
90 NEXT I
100 END
```

4. 10 INPUT "FIRST NAME",A$

```
20 INPUT "LAST NAME",B$
30 LET C$=LEFT$(A$,1)
40 PRINT C$;B$
50 END
```

5. 10 INPUT A$

```
20 FOR I=1 TO LEN(A$)
30 PRINT MID$(A$,I,1),
40 NEXT I
50 END
```

6. 10 PRINT "1 . PRINT LETTERS FROM LEFT OF STRING"

```
20 PRINT "2. PRINT LETTERS FROM RIGHT OF STRING"
30 INPUT "ENTER CHOICE",C
40 INPUT A$
50 INPUT "HOW MANY CHARACTERS",N
60 IF C=1 THEN PRINT LEFT$(A$,N):GOTO 80
70 IF C=2 THEN PRINT RIGHT$(A$,N)
80 END
```

7. 10 INPUT A$

```
20 FOR I=1 TO LEN(A$)
30 C$=MID$(A$,I,1)
40 IF C$="a" or C$="e" OR C$="i" OR C$="o" OR C$="U" THEN W$=W$+"$"
50 IF C$=" " THEN W$=w$+"@"
60 IF C$!="a" or C$!="e" or C$!="i" C$!="o" OR C$!="U" then W$=W$+(C$+2)
70 NEXT I
80 PRINT W$
90 END
```

8. 10 INPUT A$

```
20 FOR I=1 TO LEN(A$)
30 FOR K=1 TO I
40 PRINT " ";
```

```
50 NEXT K
60 FOR J=I TO L
70 PRINT MID$(A$,J,1);
80 NEXT J
90 PRINT
100 NEXT I
110 END
```

9.

```
10 INPUT N$

20 FOR I=1 TO LEN(N$)
30 C$=MID$(N$,I,1)
40 IF C$="A" OR C$="E" OR C$="I" OR C$="O" OR C$="U" THEN W$=W$+CHR$(ASC(C$)+2)) ELSE W$=W$+C$
50 NEXT I
60 PRINT W$
70 END
```

About The Centre

CENTRE OF COMPUTER TECHNOLOGY

Offers courses like

1. CERTIFICATE IN OFFICE AUTOMATION
2. DIPLOMA IN COMPUTER STUDIES
3. DIPLOMA IN JAVA PROGRAMMING
4. DIPLOMA IN DOT NET TECHNNOLOGY
5. FULL STACK WEB DEVELOPMENT

VARIOUS SHORT TERM COURSES ALSO
YOU CAN CONTACT ON
jashpritma@gmail.com

9 798886 291995

Printed by Libri Plureos GmbH in Hamburg,
Germany